THE SEVEN LETTERS

COMMENTARY ON REVELATION 2 & 3

THE SEVEN LETTERS

COMMENTARY ON REVELATION 2 & 3

AARON ERHARDT

EP

ERHARDT PUBLICATIONS

Louisville, Kentucky
2008

DEDICATION

To my dad, Douglas Jay Erhardt.
He was more than just my dad; he was my best friend.
Although there are many great things that I could say about
him, the most important is that he was baptized
into Christ on the 16th day of February 1997.
He then led me and others to do the same.

ALSO DEDICATED TO

Randy Case
Darrell West
Larry Stevens

CONTENTS

FOREWORD

Jesus, the master teacher, should be our pattern in proclaiming God's message. In his stirring letters to the seven churches of Asia, the Savior was very direct. He did not generalize. In contrast, many voices today call for us to bring general messages that will not offend anyone. However, Christ was quite direct, and his letters specified the many errors and failings of these early churches. He was not afraid to call upon them to make corrections. Should we do any less?

The letters to the seven churches of Asia reveal conditions that can be found in every congregation of the Lord's people. The letters show a complete picture of general conditions facing these seven New Testament churches, and yet they are still representative of possible conditions in all churches throughout time. For this reason, the author's book provides a practical treatment needed by disciples of our Lord today.

My friend and fellow evangelist, Aaron Erhardt, has an exceptional ability for teaching and preaching the gospel of Christ. Though still young in years, Aaron has a maturity of heart and spirit that belies his age. His zeal and godly enthusiasm bolsters the faith of all who hear him preach. His writings are clear, concise, and easy for every reader to understand. He is not afraid to press the necessary applications in our Lord's messages that we need the most today. This is the honesty and candor we need in our congregations and in our work for Christ!

Aaron has been meticulous and careful in his research of the times and places of the first century. While scholarly in approach and treatment, each study of the seven churches is still very readable. Preachers and teachers will be able to use this work as a profitable reference for classroom instruction, sermon material, home studies, and private reading.

One of the most helpful parts of this book will be found in the last chapter entitled "Closing Thoughts." Here the author makes several applications for churches of our own day. Aaron's observations are not only thought provoking, but they also challenge each reader to make personal application of the truths found in the seven letters. Aaron's thoughts about tolerance, church discipline, and dealing with issues are especially ones needed in congregations today.

I am delighted to write the foreword to this good book and to encourage its reception and reading. I am confident that those who read this work will be greatly strengthened and blessed. All of us who read, hear, and keep the words of the original author have a promised blessing (Revelation 1:3). We will also be thankful to this human author who has placed such a helpful study guide into our hands.

Bob Dickey

ASIA MINOR

Pergamos

Thyatira

Sardis

Philadelphia

Smyrna

Ephesus

Laodicea

Aegean Sea

Sea of Crete

Mediterranean Sea

INTRODUCTION

Near the end of the first century, the Lord Jesus, through John the apostle, wrote letters to seven churches that existed in Asia (modern-day Turkey). The churches were located in Ephesus, Smyrna, Pergamos, Thyatira, Sardis, Philadelphia, and Laodicea. These letters were sent to *actual* churches and addressed *actual* conditions within the churches. They are, however, representative of all churches in any age and have a universal application.

A careful analysis of the letters leads to the conclusion that all conditions ever to be found in a congregation of the Lord's church at any time in history may be found, at least in principle, in one or more of these seven churches. This makes the letters practical and worthy of study for all time (Hailey, p. 118).

The letters to the seven churches of Asia are both inspiring and sobering. They remind us that Jesus truly is "the chief Shepherd" (1 Peter 5:4) who walks among the churches inspecting them with a close eye (Revelation 1:13; 2:1). *He is watching!* His deep concern for the spiritual vitality of the churches in the face of impending persecution is evident. There are stern words of rebuke (when necessary) followed by reassuring promises of reward to those who overcome.

Some have wondered why the Lord only wrote to seven of the churches when others existed in the region, including

Troas, Colossae, and Hierapolis (Acts 20:7; Colossians 1:2; 4:13), and possibly Magnesia and Tralles since Ignatius of Antioch wrote letters to those churches in the second century. We simply do not know. It may have something to do with the fact that seven is the "perfect number" in the book of Revelation, representing completeness or fullness. These seven churches sufficiently represent the various conditions that may be found in a congregation at any time.

These letters provide us with a glimpse into the conditions of the early churches. We see their strengths and weaknesses, highs and lows, virtues and vices. There are things they did well and things they did not do well. In them, we see us!

ENVIRONMENT

The letters to the seven churches of Asia were written at about A. D. 95-96. At that time, Rome was the world-ruling empire, and Domitian was the reigning emperor. He reigned from A. D. 81-96. Domitian imposed a state-religion upon the people in the form of emperor worship. Emperor worship involved burning a pinch of incense and saying that Caesar was Lord. Those who fulfilled their ceremonial obligations were issued a certificate good for one year while those who refused to do so were accused of treason and severely persecuted. Obviously this made life very difficult for Christians since they honored Jesus Christ as Lord (1 Corinthians 12:3), not Caesar.

Once a year everyone in the empire had to appear before Domitian's magistrates to say *kaisar kurios,* Caesar is Lord, and as a testimony, to burn a pinch of incense to the godhead of Caesar. After this loyalty test, a written certificate good for one year was issued (McCord, p. 13).

Emperor Domitian (A. D. 51-96)

Born: October 24, 51   Wife: Domitia
Birthplace: Rome   Reign: 81-96
Father: Vespasian   Died: September 18, 96
Mother: Domitilla

Domitian became emperor of Rome when his older brother, Titus, died. Domitian was only 30 years old.

Domitian was a cruel and paranoid emperor. He punished anyone he suspected of having divided loyalties, including family members. Domitian was murdered by a man named Stephanus. His wife, Domitia, was involved in the plot.

Although Christians in the first century willingly submitted to the emperor's civil authority (Romans 13:1-7), they could not worship him as a god. In such cases, they had to "obey God rather than men" (Acts 5:29). The consequences of that decision were often severe.

To the Romans the refusal to worship the emperor was a sign of disloyalty to the State and an act of treason... Many Christians were beheaded, some were exiled, and others had all their property confiscated and were reduced to poverty (Summers, pp. 92, 93)

In addition to emperor worship, Christians faced other obstacles. They were constantly being pressured by their pagan neighbors to participate in temple festivals, and they were reviled by the unbelieving Jews, who were perhaps the strongest opponents of Christianity at that time. Of course, Satan was behind it all (Revelation 2:9-10, 13; 3:9).

Christians often lived as social outcasts in the province of Asia. Because they refused to participate in the evils around them, they faced tension and turmoil on a regular basis. This type of environment serves as the backdrop for the seven letters!

ANGELS

Each of the seven letters is addressed to the "angel of the church" (2:1, 8, 12, 18; 3:1, 7, 14). The word angel (*angelos*) means messenger, and it could refer to either a heavenly or human messenger, or it could symbolically refer to something else. This writer believes that the angel symbolically personified the internal spirit of the church — the sum total of its spiritual existence. This seems most reasonable since each letter is addressed to the angel of the church and concludes with the admonition, "He that hath an ear, let him hear what the Spirit saith unto the churches," suggesting that the angel and church are one and the same. The language within the letters lends support to this view as well. Consider the passages below.

"Unto the angel of the church in Smyrna write... the devil shall cast some of you into prison" (2:8, 10).

"Unto the angel of the church in Thyatira write... I will give unto every one of you according to your works" (2:18, 23).

Other views include: (1) The angel was the human messenger who took the letter to the church from John. (2) The angel was the eldership of the church. (3) The angel was the evangelist of the church. (4) The angel was the heavenly messenger assigned to the church as its guardian.

LAYOUT

Each of the seven letters follow the same sevenfold pattern, with a few exceptions along the way: (1) *Commission:* "Unto the angel of the church in [city] write..." (2) *Character:* "These things saith he that..." (3) *Commendation:* "I know thy works..." (4) *Condemnation:* "I have a few things against thee..." (5) *Correction:* "Repent..." (6) *Call:* "He that hath an ear, let him hear..." (7) *Challenge:* "He that overcometh..." It is hard to tell how much significance should be attached to the fact that the seven letters follow a sevenfold pattern.

It is difficult to know how much symbolic weight should be assigned to the sevenfold outline...it is likely that some significance should be attached, especially since there are seven churches and seven parts; probably this number emphasizes that these letters provide the perfect message from God for these churches (Osborne, p. 106).

The Lord begins each letter by commissioning John to "write" (2:1, 8, 12, 18; 3:1, 7, 14). He then dictates to the apostle what to write. Sometimes the apostles used this same kind of arrangement when writing their epistles (Romans 16:22; 1 Peter 5:12). *John wrote, but Jesus authored!*

The Lord identifies himself at the beginning of each letter using descriptive language, much of which is taken from chapter 1. He refers to himself in the third person, never using his personal name (Jesus). In fact, his personal name does not appear at all in any of the seven letters. Furthermore, these self-descriptions are often closely related to the situation that existed in each church and its surroundings.

SELF-DESCRIPTIONS

Ephesus
These things saith he that holdeth the seven stars in his right hand, who walketh in the midst of the seven golden candlesticks (2:1).

Smyrna
These things saith the first and the last, which was dead, and is alive (2:8).

Pergamos
These things saith he which hath the sharp sword with two edges (2:12).

Thyatira
These things saith the Son of God, who hath his eyes like unto a flame of fire, and his feet are like fine brass (2:18).

Sardis
These things saith he that hath the seven Spirits of God, and the seven stars (3:1).

Philadelphia
These things saith he that is holy, he that is true, he that hath the key of David, he that openeth, and no man shutteth; and shutteth, and no man openeth (3:7).

Laodicea
These things saith the Amen, the faithful and true witness, the beginning of the creation of God (3:14).

PROMISES TO THOSE WHO OVERCOME

Ephesus   To him that overcometh will I give to eat of the tree of life, which is in the midst of the paradise of God (2:7).

Smyrna   He that overcometh shall not be hurt of the second death (2:11).

Pergamos   To him that overcometh will I give to eat of the hidden manna, and will give him a white stone, and in the stone a new name written, which no man knoweth saving he that receiveth it (2:17).

Thyatira   He that overcometh, and keepeth my works unto the end, to him will I give power over the nations: and he shall rule them with a rod of iron; as the vessels of a potter shall they be broken to shivers: even as I received of my Father. And I will give him the morning star (2:26-28).

Sardis   He that overcometh, the same shall be clothed in white raiment; and I will not blot out his name out of the book of life, but I will confess his name before my Father, and before his angels (3:5).

Philadelphia   Him that overcometh will I make a pillar in
the temple of my God, and he shall go no
more out: and I will write upon him the
name of my God, and the name of the city
of my God, which is new Jerusalem, which
cometh down out of heaven from my God:
and I will write upon him my new name
(3:12).

Laodicea   To him that overcometh will I grant to sit
with me in my throne, even as I also
overcame, and am set down with my Father
in his throne (3:21).

In the King James Version, there are three phrases that appear in all seven letters. The first phrase appears at the beginning of the letters while the other two phrases appear near the end. They are significant and need to be considered carefully.

(1) *"I know thy works"* (2:2, 9, 13, 19; 3:1, 8, 15). "Know" comes from the Greek word *oida*, and refers, in this context, to absolute or certain knowledge. The Lord reminds each church that he has an accurate understanding of what is going on there. *His information is firsthand!* He is omniscient; nothing is concealed from his sight. His assessment of the churches is infallible. "Works" implicitly refutes the denominational concept that works and salvation are antagonistic. The Lord will judge us based on our works (2 Corinthians 5:10).

(2) *"He that hath an ear, let him hear"* (2:7, 11, 17, 29; 3:6, 13, 22). This is a call for each member of the church to heed what has been said. *To hear is to obey!* The threats are real; the consequences severe. The Lord made similar statements during his earthly ministry (Matthew 11:15; 13:9, 43; Mark 4:9, 23; Luke 8:8; 14:35). There is certainly a sense of prophetic warning in these words.

(3) *"To him [he] that overcometh"* (2:7, 11, 17, 26; 3:5, 12, 21). "Overcome" comes from the Greek word *nikao*, and refers to one who is victorious; a conqueror. In fact, the same word is rendered "conquer" in 6:2.

Those who heed what has been said and prevail over the circumstances they are facing will be blessed with eternal life in heaven. As conquerors, they will be rewarded!

These are the ones who maintain their witness and walk with Jesus in the midst of internal pressure from the false teachers and external persecution from the Jews and Romans (Osborne, p. 43).

It is interesting to note that the exhortation is before the promise in the first three letters, while the promise is before the exhortation in the last four letters.

ORDER

There does not seem to be any special reason for the order in which the seven letters appear, other than basic geography. If one were traveling from Patmos (where the letters were written) he would come first to Ephesus. He would then make his way up the coast and back down finishing up in Laodicea. It is worth noting that Ephesus was the most important of the seven cities.

PATMOS

Patmos was a small island located about 65-70 miles southwest of Ephesus in the Aegean Sea. At its extremities, Patmos was 10 miles long and 6 miles wide. It was barren and rocky. During the reign of Domitian, John was banished to Patmos "for the word of God, and for the testimony of Jesus Christ" (1:9). Supposing that John was banished as a criminal, it is quite possible that the aged apostle endured exhausting labor under the watchful eye of a Roman authority without a sufficient amount of food and clothing. Eusebius says that John was released from the island and returned to Ephesus shortly after Domitian's death.

EPHESUS

REVELATION 2:1-7

Ephesus was located in west Asia near the mouth of the Cayster River. The city was the fourth most important city in the Roman Empire behind Rome, Alexandria, and Antioch of Syria. Its population was estimated to be 250,000 or more. Ephesus enjoyed the privilege of being a free city, meaning it was self-governed and not occupied by Roman troops. Such a status was granted because of fidelity and service to Rome. Although Pergamos was the official capital of the province, the governor resided in Ephesus and the city was granted the right of first landing (*cataplous*), which required incoming Roman governors to land there when entering the province. Ephesus contended with Smyrna for the title "First of Asia."

Ephesus was known as both a religious and commercial center. It was situated at the junction of four major roads and had a harbor that could accommodate the largest ships, although river silt was a constant problem.

Along with the waters of the Cayster came significant amounts of silt that settled in the harbor and caused it to fill up gradually...Today the ruins of ancient Ephesus are more than five miles inland due to centuries of silt deposits (DeVries, p. 373)

From the harbor, visitors would travel down a broad street lined with columns and magnificent buildings to a huge theater. This street served as the main artery of the city and was illuminated with oil lamps. The street was later named the Arcadian Way in honor of Emperor Arcadius (A. D. 395-408).

Ephesus was home to one of the seven wonders of the ancient world — the temple of the goddess Artemis, also called Diana. The temple was 425 feet long and 220 feet wide, with 127 pillars that were each 60 feet high. The image of the goddess, which was believed to have fallen from the sky, stood in the center of the temple. Thousands of priestesses, who were little more than prostitutes, served in the temple and played a major role in the worship of Artemis, which was extremely chaotic and vile.

The worship of the temple was a weird, ecstatic, hysterical business. To the accompaniments of shouts and wailings, the burning of incense and the playing on the flute, the worshippers worked themselves up into an emotional and hysterical frenzy in which the darkest and most shameless things could and did happen (Barclay, p. 5).

The temple's inner shrine was so secure that it served as a bank of sorts. Large monetary deposits were kept there. The temple also possessed the right of asylum for criminals, allowing even the worst lawbreakers safe harbor if they could make it to the temple grounds without being arrested.

The temple was the foundation of the city's prosperity. People came from all around the world to worship the goddess (Acts 19:27). The temple was later destroyed by the Goths (A. D. 262-263).

In addition to Artemis, Ephesus was devoted to emporer worship, which thrived during the reign of Domitian. This made being a Christian there very difficult.

The huge theater in Ephesus seated an estimated 24,000 people. It was built on the side of Mount Pion and is still visible today. The city also had a stadium, gymnasium, and marketplace. The famous Celsus Library was not built until after the seven letters were written. Construction began on it in A. D. 110. Ephesus was famous for its games.

The church at Ephesus was established by the apostle Paul. We also know that Timothy labored in Ephesus for a time (1 Timothy 1:3), and tradition says that John spent the latter years of his life there. In addition to this letter, the Ephesian church received another letter that is recorded in the New Testament (the book of Ephesians). Ignatius of Antioch also wrote to the church at Ephesus in the second century.

The Christians at Ephesus were externally sound but internally shallow. They were giving the Lord their service but not their heart. Therefore, he charged them with having "left" their first love (2:4).

2:1) Unto the angel of the church of Ephesus write; These things saith he that holdeth the seven stars in his right hand, who walketh in the midst of the seven golden candlesticks.

The Lord addresses each of the seven letters to the angel of the local church. **Angel** means messenger, and it could refer to either a heavenly or human messenger, or it could symbolically refer to something else. This writer believes that the angel symbolically personified the internal spirit of the church; the sum total of its spiritual existence (see Introduction). **These things saith** appears in all seven letters, and sets a strong and authoritative tone for what is about to be said. This phrase *(tade legei)* appears only one other time in the New Testament (Acts 21:11). The Lord also begins each of the seven letters with a self-description, which serves to authorize the commands given. In this letter he describes himself as the one who holds the seven stars in his right hand and walks in the midst of the seven golden candlesticks (see 1:13, 16). **Holdeth** indicates authority. They are under his power. He controls their destiny. This image may also be one of protection (John 10:29). This affirms his omnipotence. **Walketh** indicates presence. The Lord is with them. He is examining and inspecting their activities. His presence is not confined to any one church; he is with them all. This affirms his omnipresence. **Seven stars** are the angels of the seven churches (1:20). **Seven golden candlesticks** are the seven churches (1:20). The churches are called candlesticks (lit: lampstands) because they are light-bearers. They hold up the light of the gospel and dispel darkness.

It is interesting to note that whereas the glorified Christ is depicted in chapter 1 as being "in the midst" of the churches (v. 13), now he is said to be *"walking in the midst"* of the churches. The meaning is no doubt the same, but a bit more emphatic here.

2) I know thy works, and thy labor, and thy patience, and how thou canst not bear them which are evil: and thou hast tried them which say they are apostles, and are not, and hast found them liars.

The phrase **I know thy works** appears in each of the seven letters and reminds each church that the Lord has an accurate understanding of what is going on there. His knowledge is complete and infallible (Hebrews 4:13). This affirms his omniscience. **Labor** indicates toiling in spite of great difficulty to the point of exhaustion. These brethren were willing to sweat. **Patience** means endurance or perseverance. They were steadfast. **Canst not bear them which are evil** indicates intolerance on the part of the church. They would not tolerate evil men. **Tried** indicates proving or testing. This testing of the so-called apostles may have simply consisted of comparing their teachings to the truth which had previously been taught (if the word apostle is used here in a general sense) or could have consisted of testing their ability to perform and impart the miraculous gifts (if the word is used here in the special sense). The Ephesians did not lack spiritual discernment. They were able to distinguish between truth and error. Conflicts between competing authorities were not unusual in the early church.

Ignatius of Antioch wrote a letter to the church at Ephesus in the second century in which he commended the brethren for not tolerating error. He wrote, "You all live according to truth, and no heresy has a home among you; indeed, you do not so much as listen to anyone if they speak of anything except concerning Jesus Christ in truth." So apparently their loyalty to truth continued long after this letter was written!

3) And hast borne, and hast patience, and for my name's sake hast labored, and hast not fainted.

The Lord continues commending the church for its perseverance. **Fainted** means to grow weary. *They toiled to the point of weariness without wearying of their toil!* They had not allowed discouragement to slow them down.

4) Nevertheless I have somewhat against thee, because thou hast left thy first love.

Commendation now turns to condemnation. The Ephesians had left their first love. **Left** indicates complete abandonment. **First love** is probably a reference to the love they had at the time of their conversion. The love they had at first was gone! The Ephesians had a strong mind because they were able to distinguish between truth and error. However, they had a weak heart because they no longer possessed strong love. This tragic decline often occurs gradually and without detection.

They had set out to be defenders of the faith, arming themselves with the heroic virtues of truth and courage, only to discover that in the battle they had lost the one quality without which all others are worthless (Caird, p. 31).

Approximately 30 years earlier the church at Ephesus was praised for its faithfulness and love (Ephesians 1:15-16). Now the latter was gone. This should serve as a warning to all churches of Christ as they age.

5) Remember therefore from whence thou art fallen, and repent, and do the first works; or else I will come unto thee quickly, and will remove thy candlestick out of his place, except thou repent.

The Lord calls on the Ephesians to remember their past. **Remember** indicates continued remembrance. The idea is "keep on remembering" or "hold in memory." He told the church at Sardis the same thing (3:3). Memory can be a great motivator. The prodigal son would not have returned home if it were not for his memory (Luke 15:17). **Repent** means to change one's mind and behavior. **First works** were the fruits of their first love. The two stand and fall together. "Left thy first love...do the first works." The admonition is to remember, repent, and redo. **I will come unto thee quickly** indicates impending judgment against the congregation. It is not a reference to final judgment. **Remove thy candlestick** indicates cessation of fellowship. He would no longer recognize the church as one of his own. "Repent...or else." Their options were limited — *revival or removal!*

The Ephesians had left their first love, needed to repent, and were on the verge of having their candlestick removed. Would they still be saved if their condition didn't improve? Surely not! This denies the once saved — always saved doctrine.

6) But this thou hast, that thou hatest the deeds of the Nicolaitans, which I also hate.

The Lord now returns to issuing words of commendation. The doctrinal soundness of this church was something to be admired. They were commited to upholding the truth. **Hatest** indicates abhorrence. It is much more than mere disapproval. The Ephesians absolutely abhorred the deeds of the Nicolaitans. The **Nicolaitans** were an apostate group about which little is known. Most believe that they used Christian liberty as an excuse for self-indulgence and immorality. *Christian liberty is not a license to sin!* The Nicolaitans are also mentioned in the letter to Pergamos (2:15). "Thou hatest...I also hate." Christians are to hate all forms of evil (Psalm 119:104, 128; Romans 12:9) just as Christ does. Please note, however, that we are to hate the deeds, not the people.

Irenaeus suggested that the Nicolas mentioned in Acts 6 was the founder of the Nicolaitans. Although that is an interesting thought, there is no real evidence to substantiate his claim.

The licentious behavior of the Nicolaitans had all the hallmarks of gnosticism, a heresy which flourished in the second century. Nicolaitanism was no doubt an early expression of it.

7) He that hath an ear, let him hear what the Spirit saith unto the churches; To him that overcometh will I give to eat of the tree of life, which is in the midst of the paradise of God.

The Lord concludes each of the seven letters by calling on the individual members of the church to heed what the Spirit has said (2:7, 11, 17, 29; 3:6, 13, 22) and promises them eternal life if they will do so, though the figures differ. **He that hath an ear** indicates individual responsibility. To hear is to obey. **What the Spirit saith** indicates that the Holy Spirit, the third person of the Godhead, was working in close relation with the Lord in revealing these letters (1:10; 4:2; 17:3; 21:10). He was the medium through which Christ spoke to John. Christ → Spirit → John.

In the proclamations to the seven churches in Rev 2-3, the refrain "Let the one with ears hear what the Spirit says to the churches" is repeated seven times (2:7, 11, 17, 29; 3:6, 13, 22). Since each of the proclamations is presented as the word of the exalted Christ, a close relationship between Christ and the Spirit is presupposed (Aune, p. 36).

Unto the churches indicates that each letter was to be read and applied by all seven churches, and others for that matter. *The admonitions and warning were relevant for all!* **Overcometh** is the same Greek word rendered "conquer" in 6:2. **Tree of life** is a symbolic reference to the tree in the Garden of Eden (Genesis 2:9). John describes the tree of life as being in heaven (22:2, 14). Thus the tree indicates eternal life in heaven. **Paradise** is thought to be of Persian origin, denoting beautiful gardens and parks. The paradise of God is heaven (2 Corinthians 12:2-4). The word paradise is used differently here than in Luke 23:43, where the word refers to Abraham's bosom in the hadean realm. Those who overcome, says the Spirit, will be granted eternal life in heaven with God!

Each letter begins with the Lord commissioning John to "write" and concludes with the statement "let him hear what the Spirit saith unto the churches." This indicates that the Holy Spirit *speaks* through the written Word, not separate and apart from it.

SMYRNA

REVELATION 2:8-11

Smyrna, called Izmir today, was located about 40 miles north of Ephesus on the Aegean Sea. It was a very beautiful city surrounded by rolling hills and groves of trees, with stately buildings and spacious streets. Smyrna's most famous street was "the Golden Street," which ran from one end of the city to the other. At one end of the street was the temple of Cybele and at the other end the temple of Zeus. Smyrna also had a theater which seated an estimated 20,000 people. It was situated on the side of Mount Pagos. In addition, the city had a large stadium, a medical center, and a library. It was also famous for its games. Smyrna contended with its neighbor to the south for the title "First of Asia."

Smyrna was a wealthy city, primarily because of its magnificent harbor which stimulated trade. Like Ephesus, Smyrna enjoyed the privilege of being a free city, meaning it was self-governed and not occupied by Roman troops.

Smyrna had many pagan temples. Cybele, Zeus, Apollo, Asclepius, Aphrodite, Dionysus, and other gods were worshipped there. The city, which had long been faithful to Rome, was also a hotbed for emperor worship. In fact, it was selected over several other cities as the site for the building of a temple in honor of Emperor Tiberius (A. D. 26).

There was a large Jewish segment in Smyrna that was very hostile to Christians (2:9). They were instigators who published libelous accusations against Christians and pushed for Rome to take legal action against them.

Christians in other cities had long been familiar with Jewish resentment...but at Smyrna and Philadelphia it was apparently more than usually virulent (Caird, p. 35).

Nothing is known about the establishment of the church at Smyrna. The most famous Christian of Smyrna was Polycarp, who studied under John the apostle and died a martyr. According to tradition, the proconsul offered to release him if he would reproach Christ, but Polycarp replied, "Eighty and six years have I served him, and he never once wronged me; how then shall I blaspheme my King, who hath saved me?" He was then burned at the stake. The Jews helped gather wood for the execution even though it was on the Sabbath. This shows just how hostile they really were toward Christians. Ignatius of Antioch wrote a letter to the church at Smyrna in the second century, as well as a letter to Polycarp.

The letter to Smyrna is the shortest of the seven letters. Like Philadelphia, the church did not receive any condemnation. There is no rebuke or call to repentance. That means the members were serious about their Christianity and stood firm against all forms of error.

2:8) And unto the angel of the church in Smyrna write; These things saith the first and the last, which was dead, and is alive.

The Lord begins with another self-description. In this letter he describes himself as the first and the last, which was dead and is alive (see 1:17-18). **First and the last** indicates eternality. He has always existed and will always exist. He has the same eternal attributes as God the Father and the Holy Spirit. This affirms his deity. **Which was dead, and is alive** refers to his physical death and resurrection. This description was most appropriate for the church at Smyrna because martyrdom awaited some of the members there. It was reassuring to know that Christ had also been put to death but is now alive forever more. He was well qualified to comfort them. He could sympathize with their plight.

Some commentators see a link between the Lord's self-description "which was dead, and is alive" and the city itself. Smyrna had been destroyed by the Lydians and was in ruins for more than three centuries until it was rebuilt in B. C. 290. In that sense, it was dead and now lived again.

9) I know thy works, and tribulation, and poverty, (but thou art rich) and I know the blasphemy of them which say they are Jews, and are not, but are the synagogue of Satan.

I know thy works indicates detailed knowledge of their actions. Nothing escapes his awareness. **Tribulation** indicates persecution that is so intense it crushes one to the ground.

These brethren were under extreme pressure! This persecution was probably the result of the Jews who acted as informants for the Romans when Christians failed to engage in emperor worship, from which Jews were exempt. **Poverty** denotes complete destitution. The idea is that of destitute to the point of begging. They were poorer than poor. In fact, there were two Greek words for poverty. *Penia* denotes few possessions. *Ptocheian* denotes no possessions. The latter is used here. It was not uncommon for Christians in the first century to have their homes pillaged and plundered (Hebrews 10:34). **Rich** refers to their spiritual condition. They were laying up "treasures in heaven" (Matthew 6:20) and were "rich in faith" (James 2:5). *These brethren had been robbed of everything but lost nothing!* It is interesting to note the stunning contrast between Smyrna, a poor but rich church, and Laodicea, a rich but poor church. **Blasphemy** means slander. Christ and his people were being slandered by the Jews. Jewish opposition to Christianity was not uncommon in the first century. The book of Acts is filled with examples of such opposition (7:1-8:3; 9:1-9; 13:44-52; 14:1-7, 19; 17:5-9, 13; 21:27-36). **Which say they are Jews, and are not** indicates that the Jews had a false identity. They were not who they thought they were. This refers to the Jews who rejected the gospel message. They no longer had the right to call themselves "Jews" in the sense of being God's chosen people. The same expression is found in the letter to Philadelphia (3:9). They were Jews outwardly but not inwardly; physically but not spiritually. True Jews are those circumcised in heart (Romans 2:28-29). The New Testament does not put any special significance on being a physical descendant of Abraham. The significance is always on being part of spiritual Israel (Galatians 3:26-29).

Synagogue could refer to either the place of worship or to the actual assembly itself. Obviously the latter is meant here. The Jews were a synagogue of Satan because they were doing his work (John 8:44). **Satan** means adversary. It is another name for the devil (v. 10). *Satan stood behind these Jews, not Abraham!*

> **How anyone can say that the Jews of today are still, in a very special and glorious and preeminent sense, God's people, is more than we can understand. God Himself calls those who reject the Saviour and persecute true believers "the synagogue of Satan." They are no longer His people (Hendriksen, p. 65).**

10) Fear none of those things which thou shalt suffer: behold, the devil shall cast some of you into prison, that ye may be tried; and ye shall have tribulation ten days: be thou faithful unto death, and I will give thee a crown of life.

The Lord warns the brethren in Smyrna that things would get worse before they got better. **Fear none of those things** is reminiscent of Matthew 10:28, where the Lord said, "Fear not them which kill the body, but are not able to kill the soul: but rather fear him which is able to destroy both soul and body in hell." **Devil** means slanderer. It is another name for Satan (v. 9). The devil is described in scripture as "the enemy" (Luke 10:19) who is on the prowl "seeking whom he may devour" (1 Peter 5:8). The devil, through the Roman Empire and unbelieving Jews, would persecute the brethren in a severe test of their faith. Imprisonment was usually a prelude to execution.

Imprisonment was not recognized by the law as a punishment for crime in the Greek or the Roman procedure. The state would not burden itself with the custody of criminals, except as a preliminary stage to their trial, or in the interval between trial and execution (Ramsay, p. 199)

The Devil Slanderer, Accuser

The Devil is a spirit being that opposes God and man. He is referred to in scripture in many ways, including "Satan" (Acts 5:3), "Belial" (2 Corinthians 6:15), "the wicked one" (Matthew 13:19), "the enemy" (Luke 10:19), "the prince of the power of the air" (Ephesians 2:2), "Apollyon" (Revelation 9:11), "Beelzebub" (Matthew 12:24), "the prince of this world" (John 16:11), "the tempter" (1 Thessalonians 3:5), and "the god of this world" (2 Corinthians 4:4).

The Devil is a formidable opponent. He is very powerful. There are limits to his power, however. Although he seeks to devour us (1 Peter 5:8), he can be resisted (James 4:7) and withstood (Ephesians 6:11). He is not as great as God (1 John 4:4).

Ten days indicates a full but limited period of testing. It is not to be taken literally. The Lord's warning was clear: *Prepare yourselves for a limited testing that will test you to the limit!* He does promise, however, that reward awaits the faithful. **Faithful unto death** means "to the point of death" or "even if it results in death." This was not asking anymore of them than what he had done. **Crown** comes from the Greek word *stephanos*, and it refers to a victor's crown. It was the crown (or wreath) given to champions. This crown is also mentioned in the letter to Philadelphia (3:11) and in several other books of the New Testament. There is a different Greek word for the crown of royalty *(diadema)*. Since Smyrna was famous for its games, the symbol of a victor's crown was quite appropriate.

The Lord's use of the word "crown" in this letter may also have something to do with the city itself. The acropolis on Mount Pagos gave the appearance of a crown, which became the symbol of the city.

It is important to note that the Lord did not promise to remove their difficulties. He did promise, however, that those who endured through the difficulties would be rewarded. The same is still true today.

11) He that hath an ear, let him hear what the Spirit saith unto the churches: He that overcometh shall not be hurt of the second death.

The Lord calls on each member to heed what the Spirit has said and promises them eternal life if they will do so. To hear is to obey. **Not** is emphatic in Greek, meaning "certainly not" or "not in any way." Those who overcome would certainly not be hurt by the second death. **Second death** is an expression peculiar to the book of Revelation (20:6, 14; 21:8). It does not appear in any other book of the New Testament. The second death is eternal separation from God in hell, which is called "the lake of fire" by John. Although these brethren may be hurt by the first death (physical), they will not be hurt by the second death (spiritual).

The unbeliever dies and finds another "death" awaiting him; the believer dies and finds eternal life (Summers, p. 113).

The promise in verse 10 "I will give thee a crown of life" is the same promise made in verse 11 "shall not be hurt of the second death." The only difference is that the former is worded positively, and the latter is worded negatively.

The Lord promised that the Christians who overcame would not be hurt by the second death. What about those who failed to overcome? Does that not imply that they would be hurt by it? Surely it does! This denies the once saved — always saved doctrine.

PERGAMOS

REVELATION 2:12-17

Pergamos, also called Pergamum and Pergamon, was located about 65 miles north of Smyrna and about 15 miles from the sea in the Caicus River valley. It was the farthest north of the seven cities. Today the city is called Bergama.

Pergamos had not become part of the Roman Empire by compulsion but by choice. King Attalus III willed his kingdom to the Romans just before his death in B. C. 133. This was a wise move that resulted in Pergamos being named the capital of the province of Asia.

The Lord's use of the figures "throne" and "sword" in this letter may indirectly point to the fact that Pergamos was the capital, although we cannot say for sure. Perhaps it was the Lord's way of reminding the brethren living in the capital city that he is the one with the real authority. *He reigns supreme!*

In addition to being the capital, Pergamos was known for its grand architecture, great walls, palaces, temples, and a theater which seated an estimated 10,000 people. The theater was situated on the side of a steep mountain just below the summit of the acropolis, giving spectators a panoramic view of the surroundings.

Every seat had a breath-taking view of the river valley and plain, nearly a thousand feet below. The cavea, or seating area, followed the natural contour of the acropolis rock — so this theater was taller and steeper than any other (Humble, p. 68).

Although Pergamos was not a port city or located on any major trade routes, it was still considered one of Asia's greatest cities. In fact, Pliny called it "by far the most distinguished city in Asia."

The city of Pergamos was famous for its huge library, which at one time had about 200,000 volumes and was second only to the library of Alexandria in Egypt. That's quite impressive considering each book was copied by hand! Mark Antony plundered the library and gave it to Cleopatra as a gift. Nevertheless, the city remained a center for learning.

The word "parchment" *(pergamena)* was derived from "Pergamos," which was produced in the city when papyrus could no longer be secured from Egypt. This writing material was made from the skins of various animals.

When the King of Pergamum wanted to build a library that would rival that in Alexandria, he hired the librarian from Alexandria. This infuriated the Pharaoh, who put the librarian in prison. The Pharaoh then refused to sell writing material, which was papyrus, to the King of Pergamum. So the King of Pergamum put out a challenge to his people to develop an alternate writing material, and they came

up with parchment — which is the use of animal skins for writing material. This is known as "Pergamum sheets" (Fair, p. 66).

Pergamos was thoroughly pagan. Athena, Asclepius, Dionysus, Zeus, and other pagan gods were worshipped there. Asclepius was the god of healing, and his symbol was the serpent, which still decorates medical symbols today. This was very offensive to Christians and Jews who associated the emblem with Satan. In fact, during the reign of Emperor Diocletian, some Christian stonecutters were put to death for refusing to carve an image of Asclepius. Sick people from all around the world would come to the temple complex of Asclepius in hopes of healing.

Sufferers were allowed to spend the night in the darkness of the temple. In the temple there were tame snakes. In the night the sufferer might be touched by one of these tame snakes as it glided over the ground on which he lay. The touch of the snake was held to be the touch of the god himself, and the touch was held to bring health and healing (Barclay, p. 32).

The gigantic altar of Zeus was situated on a hillside and caught the eye of everyone passing through the city. Smoke could be seen day and night coming from the altar as a rotating group of priests continually offered sacrifices. The altar has been reconstructed and is now on display at a museum in Berlin.

Asclepius and Zeus were addressed as *soter*, meaning

"savior." To Christians this would have been unbearable to hear since they honored Jesus Christ as "the Savior" (Philippians 3:20).

Pergamos was the leading center of emperor worship in the province of Asia. In fact, the city built at least three temples devoted to emperor worship. The first temple was built in honor of Augustus (B. C. 29). Then later, two more temples were built honoring Trajan and Severus.

Pergamos was a city where Caesar-worship was at its most intense, a city dedicated to glorying in the worship of Caesar. That indeed to a Christian would be nothing less than the worship of Satan. In Pergamos it was supremely perilous to be a Christian. There were cities in which danger descended on the Christians on the appointed day when the pinch of incense had to be burned, but where for the most part the Christians were left in peace for the rest of the year. But in Pergamos a Christian was in jeopardy of his life three hundred and sixty-five days in the year. The Christian in Pergamos had taken his life in his hands for the sake of his loyalty to Jesus Christ (Barclay, p. 34).

Although extreme ungodliness existed in all seven cities, Pergamos was the worst of all. It's no wonder then that the city was called "Satan's seat" (2:13). As noted before, emperor worship was most pressing in Pergamos and paganism, with all its immorality, ran rampant there.

Nothing is known about the establishment of the church at Pergamos. From this letter, it is evident that the church was externally strong but internally weak. Although the members resisted persecution from without, they tolerated error from within.

2:12) And to the angel of the church in Pergamos write; These things saith he which hath the sharp sword with two edges.

The Lord begins with another self-description. In this letter he describes himself as the one having the sharp sword with two edges (see 1:16). This is the simplest description of all seven letters, containing just one element. **Sharp sword with two edges** refers to God's Word, and the fact that Christ will use it in executing judgment. **Sharp** suggests the effectiveness or power of God's Word. This sword is not held in his hand but comes out of his mouth (1:16; 2:16). The sword is also mentioned in 19:15, 21.

"Sword" comes from the Greek word *rhomphaia,* and refers to a long and heavy battle sword. It is different from the Greek word translated sword in Ephesians 6:17 and Hebrews 4:12. The word in those passages is *machaira,* and refers to a short dagger-like sword (16 inches or shorter).

Pergamos was a city which had been given the rare power of capital punishment by Rome. This was known as the right of the sword *(ius gladii),* and it was symbolized by a sword. That is probably a significant factor as to why the Lord describes himself as having the sharp sword with two edges in this letter. *No Roman sword could compare to the sword of the Lord!*

> The Roman governor of Asia exercised the *ius gladii*, or right of the sword, from his bench of judgment in Pergamum. In the province he represented the authority of the emperor, who himself carried a sword or dagger as a symbol of his office. The governor's power to render capital punishment gave him the right of life and death in his jurisdiction...By using the epithet in the message to Pergamum, Jesus establishes his preeminence, even over the Roman governor (Zondervan, p. 265, 267).

The phrase "church...in Pergamos" is a tremendous paradox, which shows the power of Christ and the gospel. Although the city was given over to wickedness and even called "Satan's seat," there was still a light shining through the smog of sin!

13) I know thy works, and where thou dwellest, even where Satan's seat is: and thou holdest fast my name, and hast not denied my faith, even in those days wherein Antipas was my faithful martyr, who was slain among you, where Satan dwelleth.

I know thy works indicates detailed knowledge of their actions. Nothing escapes his awareness. **Where thou dwellest** indicates familiarity with their surroundings. He knew their plight. **Seat** means throne. The same word is used elsewhere to refer to the throne of God. **Satan's seat** is a figurative expression indicating strong influence. *Satan had free reign in Pergamos!* Pergamos was the leading center of emperor worship in the province of Asia and home to many pagan gods (See introductory notes on Pergamos). **My name** refers to the person of Christ and encompasses his authority and lordship. The brethren in Pergamos remained loyal to the name of Christ in contrast to the name of Caesar. They stood firm and did not deny him. **Antipas** was a Christian who was put to death for his faith in Christ. This may have been the result of his refusal to engage in emperor worship. **Martyr** refers to one who bears witness — in this case by his death. The term *martus* did not come to mean "martyr" as we think of it until the third century. Before that time, it simply meant witness. According to tradition, Antipas was roasted in a red-hot brazen bull during the reign of Domitian. The Lord called Antipas his "faithful witness" (ESV), which are the same words applied to Christ himself in 1:5. Apparently Antipas' death was a very difficult time for the church. **Where Satan dwelleth** identifies Pergamos as the place where Antipas was martyred, and again indicates the strong influence Satan possessed there. *It was as if Pergamos was Satan's hometown!*

Although Antipas is the only Christian mentioned by name as having been slain in Pergamos, it would be wrong to assume that he was the lone martyr. There were certainly other martyrs. Eusebius later named Carpus, Papylus, and Agathonike as martyrs in Pergamos.

His name is mentioned and preserved only as the first in the already long series. The subsequent chapters of Revelation, which tell of the woman

drunk with the blood of the saints, show what
were the real facts. That one name should stand as
representative of the whole list is entirely in the style
of the Apocalypse (Ramsey, p. 218).

14) But I have a few things against thee, because
thou hast there them that hold the doctrine of Balaam, who
taught Balak to cast a stumbling block before the children
of Israel, to eat things sacrificed unto idols, and to commit
fornication.

Commendation now turns to condemnation. The
spirit of compromise was very much alive in the church at
Pergamos, not from without but from within. Their problem
was internal. **Balaam** was a prophet in the Old Testament
who taught Balak to entice the children of Israel to eat things
sacrificed to idols and to commit fornication (Numbers 25:1-
6; 31:16). Apparently some in the congregation were teaching
that Christians could attend the pagan festivals in the city
and embrace the temple prostitutes. Fornication was quite
prevalent at that time.

In the ancient world sexual morals were loose;
relationships outside marriage were entirely accepted
and produced no stigma whatsoever (Barclay, p. 39).

Stumbling block means snare or trap. It was the
part of the trap where the bait was placed. The idea is that
of a death trap. By participating in these sinful activities,
the brethren were entering a death trap! The issue of eating
things sacrificed to idols and committing fornication had

been addressed years earlier at the Jerusalem meeting (Acts 15:29). Two other passages in the New Testament mention the negative example of Balaam (2 Peter 2:15; Jude 11).

The doctrine of Balaam in Pergamos was very similar to the doctrine of Jezebel in Thyatira, if not exactly the same. Both teachings involved eating things sacrificed to idols and committing fornication (2:14, 20).

Since emperor worship was so prevalent in Pergamos, the Balaamites may have taught that Christians could participate in that sinful activity as well.

15) So hast thou also them that hold the doctrine of the Nicolaitans, which thing I hate.

There were also some in the congregation who held to the doctrine of the Nicolaitans. The **Nicolaitans** were an apostate group about which little is known. Most believe that they used Christian liberty as an excuse for self-indulgence and immorality. *Christian liberty is not a license to sin!* Whereas the Ephesians hated this doctrine (2:6), some at Pergamos held to it. Though the doctrine of the Nicolaitans was no doubt akin to the doctrine of Balaam (both encouraged compromise with error), the language indicates that they were not identical.

(16) Repent; or else I will come unto thee quickly, and will fight against them with the sword of my mouth.

The Lord will not tolerate the spirit of compromise within the church. Therefore, he gives them a warning:

"Repent or else" (see also 2:5). **Repent** means to change one's mind and behavior. **I will come unto thee quickly** indicates impending judgment against the congregation, especially the apostate element. "I will...fight against *them*" (emp. mine). It is not a reference to final judgment. **Fight against them with the sword of my mouth** refers to judgment at the hands of truth. *Christ has the sharp sword with two edges and is about to use it!*

(17) He that hath an ear, let him hear what the Spirit saith unto the churches; To him that overcometh will I give to eat of the hidden manna, and will give him a white stone, and in the stone a new name written, which no man knoweth saving he that receiveth it.

The Lord calls on each member to heed what the Spirit has said and promises them eternal life if they will do so. To hear is to obey. **Eat of** means to share in. The **hidden manna** may have reference to the manna hidden in the Ark of the Covenant by Moses (Exodus 16:33-34). That manna was a constant reminder of how God provided for his people and sustained them physically. The idea here then is that those who overcome will be spiritually sustained in heaven. Those who abstain from the food of idols will be compensated with the food of heaven. It could also be a reference to Christ "*the bread of life*" (John 6:35), whose blessings are hidden from unbelievers.

Jewish tradition held that this manna had been miraculously preserved and would be multiplied to

feed God's people when the Messiah came (Easley, p. 39).

White stone may have reference to the practice in some ancient courts of law where the accused was condemned by black stones and acquitted by white ones. *Christians in Pergamos may stand condemned in the Roman courts but will be vindicated in the courts of heaven!* Other interpretations include: (1) White stones were given to winners of athletic competitions. Therefore, this stone indicates victory. (2) White stones were given to men freed from slavery. Therefore, this stone indicates citizenship. (3) White stones were used as tickets of admission to certain functions. Therefore, this stone indicates admittance. **In** should be translated "on" *(epi).* The new name will be written on the stone. **New** is from the Greek word *kainos,* and refers to new in the sense of being qualitatively different, not new in contrast to what is old. **Name** indicates acceptance or belonging. We do not know what the new name will be until it is received.

THYATIRA

REVELATION 2:18-29

Thyatira was located about 40 miles southeast of Pergamos. The city was situated just about halfway between Pergamos and Sardis, at the mouth of a long valley which connected the valleys of the Hermus and Caicus rivers. Today the city is called Akhisar.

Thyatira was founded as a military outpost by Seleucus I, one of Alexander the Great's successors. When it came under Roman rule, the city became a flourishing commercial center.

Thyatira was a wealthy city. This was due in large part to its location along major trade routes and the presence of the madder root, from which beautiful dye was made. Thyatira also prospered from its production of wool.

Thyatira was notorious for its trade guilds. Guilds were organized for leather-workers, wool-workers, linen-workers, dress-makers, slave-traders, bakers, dyers, potters, tanners, and nearly all other occupations. Guilds were similar to trade unions today except each guild was inseparably entwined with paganism. In other words, each guild practiced idolatrous rites at their functions. The trade guilds probably presented the biggest problem for Christians in Thyatira.

Thyatira was an industrial center controlled by guilds, that is, trade unions. These guilds paid homage to the pagan gods Apollo and Artemis (also known as Tyrimnos), and they worshiped at the shrine of Sabbathe. Members of the guild were obligated to attend festivals in honor of these gods, to eat meals in their temples, and to indulge in sexual promiscuity. Noncompliance with these rules meant expulsion from the trade union, lack of employment, and poverty. Christians who refused to honor pagan gods, eat meat sacrificed to an idol, and engage in sexual immorality jeopardized their material necessities. They were regarded as outcasts of society (Kistemaker, p. 136).

Unlike many of the other cities, Thyatira was not an important religious center. The chief god in the city was Apollo, the sun god. There was also a small Jewish segment there, although it does not appear from the letter that they posed much of a threat to Christians.

Although Thyatira was the least significant of the seven cities, the letter to the church there is the longest of the seven. That is probably because of the great amount of destruction Jezebel and her disciples were causing by teaching that it was acceptable to be members of the guilds and participate in the various pagan festivals.

Nothing is known about the establishment of the church at Thyatira. Some suggest that Lydia was responsible for planting the church there (Acts 16:14), although there is no real evidence to support that.

The comparison between Thyatira and Ephesus is quite interesting. Whereas Thyatira was commended for her love but condemned for tolerating error, Ephesus was condemned for her lack of love but commended for not tolerating error.

2:18) And unto the angel of the church in Thyatira write; These things saith the Son of God, who hath his eyes like unto a flame of fire, and his feet are like fine brass.

The Lord begins with another self-description. In this letter he describes himself as the Son of God with eyes like flaming fire and feet like fine brass (see 1:14-15). **Son of God** indicates deity. This is the only time that title occurs in the book of Revelation, and is the summation of the description of Jesus Christ in the first chapter. Whereas in chapter 1 Jesus is called "the Son of man," emphasizing his humanity, he is now called "the Son of God," emphasizing his deity. **Eyes like unto a flame of fire** indicates knowledge or insight. The Lord's eyes are penetrating so that nothing is disguised or hidden from him (v. 23). This affirms his omniscience. **Feet like fine brass** indicates strength. The Lord's feet are solid and able to crush the wicked. This affirms his omnipotence.

Apollo, the chief god in the city, was believed to be the son of Zeus, and was therefore called "the son of god." This may be why Jesus chose the title "Son of God" here. It is Jesus, not Apollo, who is the true Son of God!

It could also be that Jesus chose the title "Son of God" with the Roman emperors in mind. Emperors sometimes claimed to be "sons of god" in their official letters. A letter from Augustus to Ephesus begins "Emperor Caesar, son of god Julius."

Some commentators see a link between the Lord's portrayal as barefoot in this self-description and Roman statuary, which often depicted emperors barefoot as a sign of their divinity.

19) I know thy works, and charity, and service, and faith, and thy patience, and thy works; and the last to be more than the first.

I know thy works indicates detailed knowledge of their actions. Nothing escapes his awareness. Charity comes from the Greek word *agape,* and refers to a love that goes beyond emotion and seeks the highest good for others. **Service** refers to their willingness to assist or minister to others. Service is the fruit of love. **Faith** comes from the Greek word *pista,* meaning "fidelity" or "faithfulness." The idea is that of loyalty. **Patience** indicates lasting endurance or perseverance. **Works** is mentioned a second time because their works had increased over time. *They were growing!*

The progress of the Thyatiran church is worthy of our admiration. Their works were steadily improving with time. Unfortunately, such is not always the case in churches of Christ.

The tendency is to lose enthusiasm as time goes by and do less instead of more, but the church in Thyatira was doing more for the Lord each day (Roper, p. 143).

20) Notwithstanding I have a few things against thee, because thou sufferest that woman Jezebel, which calleth herself a prophetess, to teach and to seduce my servants to commit fornication, and to eat things sacrificed unto idols.

Commendation now turns to condemnation. The church at Thyatira tolerated error in their midst. **Sufferest** means to allow or tolerate. **Jezebel** was the wife of King Ahab in the Old Testament who stirred him to do evil (1 Kings 21:25). The Lord refers to the immoral woman in Thyatira as Jezebel because she was behaving like her. The woman's name was not really Jezebel. **Which calleth herself** indicates deception. She professed to be something she was not. Although there were legitimate prophetesses in the early church (Acts 21:9), Jezebel was not one of them. Apparently Jezebel taught that it was acceptable to commit fornication and to eat things sacrificed to idols, which were common practices at the functions guild members were obligated to attend. She argued for compromise and conformity with evil.

For persons to maintain their livelihood, some connection, indeed membership, in the guilds was a virtual necessity. For Christians the problem was that this mandated participation in the guild feasts, which themselves involved "meat offered to idols," since patron gods of the guilds were always

worshiped at the feasts...at times this could also involve immorality...Jezebel probably "taught" that there was nothing wrong with a Christian taking part in the guild feasts and celebrations, for it was merely civil (Osborne, p. 157).

Instead of tolerating Jezebel, the Thyatirans should have expelled her from their midst (1 Corinthians 5:9-11; 2 Thessalonians 3:6; Titus 3:10). As a false teacher, she should have been marked and avoided (Romans 16:17).

This is now the second time we read about churches having to deal with liars claiming to be something they are not. The Ephesians had those "claiming" to be apostles (2:2), and now the Thyatirans had a woman "claiming" to be a prophetess. These examples personify the Lord's warning in Matthew 7:15 — *"Beware of false prophets, which come to you in sheep's clothing, but inwardly they are ravening wolves!"*

21) And I gave her space to repent of her fornication; and she repented not.

Space means time. Despite her destructive ways, the Lord had been patient with Jezebel. He had given her opportunity to repent. The implication seems to be that she had been warned to repent before. **Repent** means to change one's mind and behavior. **Fornication** may refer to the physical act itself, of which she was certainly guilty, or it could refer to the fact that she was committing spiritual fornication by claiming to be a Christian while engaging in the pagan festivals. **She repented not** means she refused to change her wicked ways.

This verse highlights the longsuffering of God. He truly is "not willing that any should perish, but that all should come to repentance" (2 Peter 3:9). This does not guarantee, however, that we will always be given enough time to make correction. Ananias and Sapphira died immediately when they sinned with no opportunity to repent of their sins (Acts 5:1-11).

22) Behold I will cast her into a bed, and them that commit adultery with her into great tribulation, except they repent of their deeds.

Jezebel was running out of time! **Cast** means to throw. **Bed** probably refers to a bed of affliction or suffering — "sickbed" (ESV) "bed of sickness" (NASB) "bed of suffering" (NIV) "bed of pain" (NEB). **Them that commit adultery with her** refer to those who actively participate in the sinful activities. The suffering here is different than in other letters because it would not be *for* Christ but *because* of Christ. **Except they repent** indicates there is still time to make correction. The window of opportunity was closing, however. This was the final warning.

23) And I will kill her children with death; and all the churches shall know that I am he which searcheth the reins and hearts: and I will give unto every one of you according to your works.

Kill may or may not be literally. **Children** refer to her spiritual offspring. These are those who condoned her sinful activities. They had wholly committed themselves to Jezebel's doctrine. **All the churches shall know** indicates widespread knowledge. God's destruction of Jezebel and her disciples would serve as a warning to surrounding congregations just as God's destruction of Egypt served as a warning to surrounding nations! **Searcheth** means examine or scrutinize. The allusion here is to Jeremiah 17:10. The Lord, who has eyes like unto a flame of fire, gazes into the inner man and perceives his very feelings and thoughts. **Reins** (lit: kidneys) denotes the center of deepest emotions. Newer versions say "minds." **Hearts** denotes the center of deepest intellect. *Nothing is hidden from the Lord!* This further confirms his deity.

24) But unto you I say, and unto the rest in Thyatira, as many as have not this doctrine, and which have not known the depths of Satan, as they speak; I will put upon you none other burden.

The rest in Thyatira are those who have not participated in or condoned the error previously mentioned. **The depths of Satan** is an expression that could be interpreted two ways: (1) This was the actual terminology that Jezebel and her disciples used. If this interpretation is correct, they probably taught they could plumb the depths of Satan (by participating in the idolatrous practices of the guilds) without being scathed spiritually. (2) This was a form of sarcasm in which the Lord changes "God" to "Satan," just as he did with the synagogue of the Jews (2:9; 3:9). The belief that one could sin with impunity can be identified with gnosticism, a heresy which flourished in the second century. This doctrine was no doubt an early expression of it. **None other burden** may point back to what has just been said about the coming judgment of Jezebel or forward to what will be said in the next verse — to hold fast.

25) But that which ye have already hold fast till I come.

Hold fast means to "keep hold of firmly." This is the same admonition given to Sardis (3:3) and Philadelphia (3:11). **Till I come** indicates impending judgment against the congregation, especially the apostate element. It is not a reference to final judgment.

26) And he that overcometh, and keepeth my works unto the end, to him will I give power over the nations:

Whereas in the first three letters the exhortation is before the promise, the Lord now reverses the order. **Keepeth** means to observe. To observe is to obey. **Unto the end** refers to the time when they finish their course (2 Timothy 4:7). There is an obvious contrast here between the Lord's works and Jezebel's works (v. 22). **Will I give power over the nations** indicates authority delegated by Christ to his followers. Since Christ rules in the absolute sense, this must be understood in some secondary sense. This promise, which is taken from Psalm 2:8-9, continues in the next verse.

27) And he shall rule them with a rod of iron; as the vessels of a potter shall they be broken to shivers: even as I received of my Father.

The Christians, who were so often oppressed by unbelievers, would one day see the roles reversed. *They would rule!* This is not to be understood as an earthly rule, for the earth will be destroyed when the Lord returns (2 Peter 3:10-12). **Rod** refers to a shepherd's rod, which serves to protect and to inflict punishment. The overcomer will share in the Lord's dominance (2 Timothy 2:12).

28) And I will give him the morning star.

The morning star is Jesus himself (22:16). He promises that those who overcome will have the privilege of living with him in heaven forever. They will be in his presence, unlike the lost (2 Thessalonians 1:9).

29) He that hath an ear, let him hear what the Spirit saith unto the churches.

The Lord calls on each member to heed what the Spirit has said and promises them eternal life if they will do so. To hear is to obey.

SARDIS

REVELATION 3:1-6

S ardis was located about 30 miles southeast of Thyatira on the edge of Mount Tmolus in the Hermus River valley. The Pactolus River, a tributary to the Hermus, ran though Sardis. Today the city is called Sart.

Sardis was a wealthy city, primarily because of its successful wool industry and the Pactolus River, which at one time contained gold dust. According to legend, Midas divested himself of the golden touch by washing his hands in the river. Situated at the junction of five different roads, Sardis also became a great trading center.

Sardis had a storied past. It was the ancient capital of Lydia and was the birthplace of modern money — the first gold and silver coins were minted there. Lydia's most famous king was Croesus, who was renowned for his wealth and inspired the expression "rich as Croesus."

The citizens of Sardis were known for their loose-living. Even among the pagans, their lifestyle was considered crude. Such immorality surely created a difficult environment for Christians.

Like other cities in Asia, Sardis was given over to

idolatry. Altars and shrines decorated the city in honor of pagan gods, the most notable being Cybele. Dionysus and Zeus were among the other gods worshipped there. The temple of Artemis (possibly Cybele) in Sardis rivaled the famous temple of Artemis in Ephesus, but it was never finished.

Emperor worship was practiced in Sardis, although it does not appear from the letter that it posed much of a problem for the church. Apparently there was not a significant Jewish threat either.

Sardis was practically destroyed by an earthquake during the reign of Emperor Tiberius (A. D. 17). This resulted in a five year exemption of taxes and large sums of financial aid to help rebuild the city from Rome. Within ten years the city had regained its former grandeur. In gratitude, the citizens of Sardis built a temple in his honor and minted a special coin bearing his image.

Nothing is known about the establishment of the church at Sardis. It may have been founded during Paul's ministry at Ephesus. There is no indication that the church had to deal with a lot of outside threats, such as emperor worship, pressure from the pagans, or reviling from the unbelieving Jews. There is no mention of any internal threats either, such as false teachers. Apparently there was no trouble without or within. Nonetheless, the church grew complacent and indifferent over time, and was pronounced "dead" by the Lord (3:1). *This undisturbed church disturbed the Lord greatly!*

Neither pagan opposition nor heretical libertinistic excesses threatened this church; it suffered from

spiritual dry rot and deadness (Lenski, p. 126).

Unlike the other letters, Sardis received condemnation before commendation. The reversal in order was no doubt due to the severity of the church's spiritual condition.

3:1) And unto the angel of the church in Sardis write; These things saith he that hath the seven Spirits of God, and the seven stars; I know thy works, that thou hast a name that thou livest, and art dead.

The Lord begins with another self-description. In this letter he describes himself as the one who has the seven Spirits of God and the seven stars (see 1:4, 16). **Seven** indicates completeness or fullness. **Seven Spirits of God** refers to the Holy Spirit. Since there is but one Holy Spirit (Ephesians 4:4), this must be understood as representing the Spirit's fullness. Christ had the fullness of the Spirit with him! The **seven stars** are the angels of the churches, which the Lord holds in his right hand (1:16, 20; 2:1). **I know thy works** indicates detailed knowledge of their actions. Nothing escapes his awareness. **Thou hast a name that thou livest, and art dead** indicates false reputation. The church was viewed by men as active and healthy when in fact it was dead. This proves that reputation (what others say about you) and character (what you really are) are not the same. This deadness may have resulted in peace with their neighbors, but it did not result in peace with God. *Apparently the church was so tactful in the community that it made no contact at all!*

Of the seven churches Sardis was among the lowest in spiritual fervor. Its accommodation to its religious environment shielded the church from persecution, for hardly anyone took notice. Its inoffensive lifestyle yielded religious peace with the world but resulted in spiritual death in the sight of God (Kistemaker, p. 149).

The Holy Spirit

The Holy Spirit is the third person of the Godhead (Acts 5:3-4). He possesses all the attributes of deity. He is eternal, omniscient, omnipotent, and omnipresent. He is referred to in scripture in many ways, including "the Spirit" (Luke 4:1), "the Spirit of God" (Genesis 1:2), "the Spirit of truth" (John 16:13), "the Spirit of the Lord" (Luke 4:18), and "the Spirit of grace" (Hebrews 10:29).

The Holy Spirit hears (John 16:13), speaks (1 Timothy 4:1), teaches (John 14:26), communes (2 Corinthians 13:14), leads (Romans 8:14), loves (Romans 15:30), comforts (Acts 9:31), testifies (John 15:26), rejoices (Luke 10:21), wills (1 Corinthians 12:11), knows (1 Corinthians 2:11), and forbids (Acts 16:7). He can be lied to (Acts 5:3), grieved (Ephesians 4:30), blasphemed (Matthew 12:31), resisted (Acts 7:51), quenched (1 Thessalonians 5:19), and despised (Hebrews 10:29). All of these characteristics affirm his personage.

The Holy Spirit is alive and active in the world today. He works through the written Word. It is his means or medium of operation.

To men the church at Sardis was appealing, but to the Lord it was appalling. This should serve as a warning to all churches of Christ that enjoy great reputations.

2) Be watchful, and strengthen the things which remain, that are ready to die; for I have not found thy works perfect before God.

Be watchful means to be alert or vigilant. Newer versions say "wake up." This admonition would be all too familiar to those living in Sardis, a city that despite its nearly impregnable location was captured twice for not watching.

When the Christians in ancient Sardis heard this verse, they remembered when Cyrus, the Persian king camped outside the city of Sardis, in 546 B.C. He camped there for months with no hope of coming inside the city because he could not breach the walls. With its strong walls, mostly natural walls, it seemed impregnable. One night, however, one of his soldiers keeping watch saw a soldier from Sardis coming down a narrow path between two parts of the wall. He had come down to retrieve a fallen helmet. They informed Cyrus of the secret path, and at 3:00 in the morning the Persian army entered the city by the same pathway, each soldier walking single file up the path. When daylight broke on the city of Sardis, the Persian army had surrounded them. They had been so sure the Persians could not get in that they had not even posted a guard!...Sardis fell again in 214 B.C. to

Antiochus the Great, in almost exactly the same way
it fell to Cyrus (West Jr., pp. 50-51).

The things that remain indicate that not all was lost.
Even the surviving remnant, however, was nearing death.
Perfect means complete. Their works had never been brought
to completion; they were left undone. They were good starters
but poor finishers! This statement probably reminded the
brethren of the temple of Artemis in the city which had never
been finished. Newer versions accurately include the word
"my" before God. This demonstrates the close relationship
that exists between the Father and Son.

**3) Remember therefore how thou hast received and
heard, and hold fast, and repent. If therefore thou shalt not
watch, I will come on thee as a thief, and thou shalt not
know what hour I will come upon thee.**

The Lord calls on the church to remember its past.
Remember indicates continued remembrance. The idea
is "keep on remembering" or "hold in memory." He told
the church at Ephesus the same thing (2:5). **How thou hast
received and heard** refers to the time of their conversion. The
same enthusiasm that characterized them when they first
encountered the gospel needed to be rekindled! **Hold fast**
means to "keep hold of firmly." **Repent** means to change one's
mind and behavior. **Watch** carries with it the idea of being
prepared. The Lord warns the brethren not to make the same
mistake the city had made by not watching. **I will come on
thee** indicates impending judgment against the congregation.
It is not a reference to final judgment. **As a thief** indicates

surprise. His coming would be unannounced, unexpected, and without warning. The Second Coming of Christ is also likened to the coming of a thief in scripture (Matthew 24:43; 1 Thessalonians 5:2; 2 Peter 3:10). The admonition is fivefold: "Be watchful...strengthen...remember...hold fast...repent."

4) Thou hast a few names even in Sardis which have not defiled their garments; and they shall walk with me in white: for they are worthy.

Names refers to people. God had a remnant in Sardis who were faithful. Each of these people were known by name to God! **Defiled** means stained or soiled. **Garments** is a metaphor for the lives of Christians. The faithful few had not been polluted by the immorality of the city or the deadness of the church. **Walketh** indicates association or fellowship. **White** indicates holiness or purity. Christ was robed in white at the transfiguration (Mark 9:3), and angels were robed in white at the resurrection (Mark 16:5) and ascension (Acts 1:10). White may also indicate victory since Roman generals wore white after victorious military campaigns. **Worthy** means entitled to. This shows that judgment is not congregational, but individual. *Since the faithful few did not "run with the pack," they would walk with the Lord!*

The Lord said there were "a few" in the congregation who had not defiled their garments, implying that the rest had. Would those Christians who defiled their garments still be saved if their condition didn't improve? Surely not! This denies the once saved — always saved doctrine.

Among the pagans, defiled garments disqualified the worshipper and dishonored the god. This may be why Jesus chose the metaphor "defiled garments" here. However, he is speaking of spiritual defilement.

5) He that overcometh, the same shall be clothed in white raiment; and I will not blot out his name out of the book of life, but I will confess his name before my Father, and before his holy angels.

The Lord promises those who overcome three things: (1) They will be clothed in white raiment. (2) They will not have their names blotted out of the book of life. (3) They will have their names confessed by Christ before the Father and his angels. **White raiment** indicates holiness or purity, and possibly victory (v. 4). **The book of life** is mentioned throughout the Bible, as well as several times in the book of Revelation (13:8; 17:8; 20:12, 15, 21:27). It metaphorically refers to the heavenly record of the faithful, the list of those who belong to God. Many ancient civilizations kept a record of its citizens. When a person died, his name was erased. The Lord promises that the names of those who overcome will never be erased. Their names are in the record and will stay there! **I will confess his name before my Father, and the holy angels** is reminiscent of the Lord's promise in Matthew 10:32 and Luke 12:8. "I will not...but I will."

The possibility of having one's name erased from the Book of Life suggests that fidelity to God rather than any type of predestinarian system is the reason

for having one's name inscribed in the Book of Life in the first place (Aune, p. 223).

In this verse the Lord promises not to blot out the names of those who overcome from the book of life. What about those who do not overcome? Does this not imply that their names will be blotted out? This denies the once saved — always saved doctrine.

6) He that hath an ear, let him hear what the Spirit saith unto the churches.

The Lord calls on each member to heed what the Spirit has said and promises them eternal life if they will do so. To hear is to obey.

PHILADELPHIA

REVELATION 3:7-13

P hiladelphia was located about 30 miles southeast of Sardis on the Cogamus River, near the edge of a great plain called "the burnt land." This plain was one of the most fertile areas in the world because of the volcanic ash that fell on it. Philadelphia served as the gateway to the East. Today the city is called Alasehir.

Philadelphia was the youngest of the seven cities of Asia. It was founded by Attalus II of Pergamos somewhere between B. C. 140-150. Attalus was so devoted to his brother, Eumenes, that he was given the nickname *Philadelphus* — brother-lover. That nickname became the name of the new city.

Philadelphia was a wealthy city, primarily because of the major trade routes that ran through the city and its great grape growing ability, from which fine wines were made. Philadelphia also had a successful leather industry. Furthermore, nearby hot springs attracted visitors from all around the world to Philadelphia.

Philadelphia was plagued with earthquakes. In fact, Strabo described the city as "full of earthquakes" and said "the walls never cease being cracked." Like Sardis, the city was practically destroyed by an earthquake during the reign of Emperor Tiberius (A. D. 17), and received a five year exemption of taxes and large sums of financial aid to help rebuild the city from Rome. In gratitude, the citizens of Philadelphia renamed the city Neocaesarea (New Caesar). The name was later changed again to Flavia. In addition to the name Philadelphia, Flavia remained throughout the second and third centuries.

The people of Philadelphia lived in constant dread of disaster, and many chose to live in rural areas outside of the city.

For a number of years the people were kept in terror by the continual tremors that plagued the area, and because of this fear much of the populace lived in huts in the adjacent countryside outside the city (Hailey, p. 149).

The city of Philadelphia was founded to spread Greek civilization eastward. It was an "open door" for the advancement of both the language and culture. This may be why the Lord used the expression "open door" in the letter to Philadelphia (3:8).

Since there were so many pagan temples there, Philadelphia was called "Little Athens." Dionysus, the god of wine, was the chief god in the city. The church, however, seems to have suffered more persecution from the unbelieving Jews than from the pagans (3:9).

Nothing is known about the establishment of the church at Philadelphia. It may have been founded during Paul's ministry at Ephesus. We do know that Ignatius of Antioch wrote a letter to the church at Philadelphia in the second century.

The church at Philadelphia proves the old adage to be true — *It's not the size of the dog in the fight but the size of the fight in the dog that counts!* Although the church had little resources, it was strong in faith.

There are several similarities between Smyrna and Philadelphia: (1) Both churches received only praise from the Lord. (2) Both churches suffered persecution at the hands of the Jews. (3) Both churches were promised a victor's crown if they remained faithful. (4) Both churches persevered despite being physically hindered. *Smyrna was the "poor but rich" church and Philadelphia was the "weak but strong" church!*

3:7) And to the angel of the church in Philadelphia write; These things saith he that is holy, he that is true, he that hath the key of David, he that openeth, and no man shutteth; and shutteth, and no man openeth.

The Lord begins with another self-description. In this letter he describes himself as holy and true, possessing the key of David, and having the ability to open and shut (Isaiah 22:22). **Holy** means sanctified or set apart from. The Lord is completely set apart from sin. He is "the Holy One." This affirms his deity. **True** means genuine or real. The idea is that of absolute truth, possibly in contrast to the false gods and false Jews in the city. He is "the True One." In chapter 6 the martyrs address God the Father as "holy and true" (v. 10). **Key** indicates authority. Whoever holds the key is in control. **David** symbolizes the messianic office. The Lord possesses the keys of salvation. He also possesses the keys of hades and death (1:18). The reference to David may have the Jewish persecutors in mind, who challenged the claim that Jesus was the promised Davidic Christ. **He that openeth, and no man shutteth; and shutteth, and no man openeth** again indicates authority. He alone has the power to permit or deny. This affirms his omnipotence.

8) I know thy works: behold, I have set before thee an open door, and no man can shut it: for thou hast a little strength, and hast kept my word, and hast not denied my name.

I know thy works indicates detailed knowledge of their actions. Nothing escapes his awareness. **Open door** indicates opportunity. This figure is used several times in scripture in reference to evangelistic opportunity (Acts 14:27; 1 Corinthians 16:9; 2 Corinthians 2:12; Colossians 4:3). The Lord would bless the church at Philadelphia with even greater opportunities to spread the gospel message. Others see this figure as referring to the open door of heaven (4:1). **No man can shut** may imply that their adversaries would try to shut it, but they would not be able to do so. **Little strength** refers to their physical condition. They were little in number and resources. Spiritually speaking, however, they were of great strength because they kept his word and did not deny his name. **Kept my word** indicates obedience. They are commended for this again in verse 10. **Not denied my name** indicates loyalty.

As mentioned before, there may be a link here between the expression "open door" and the city itself. Philadelphia had been established for the very purpose of spreading Greek culture, that it might be an open door. Now the Lord says that the church would be given an open door for spreading the gospel!

9) Behold, I will make them of the synagogue of Satan, which say they are Jews, and are not, but do lie; behold, I will make them to come and worship before thy feet, and to know that I have loved thee.

This verse is very similar to 2:9. **Synagogue** could refer to either the place of worship or to the actual assembly itself. Obviously the latter is meant here. **Satan** means adversary. **Which say they are Jews, and are not** indicates that the Jews had a false identity. They were not who they thought they were. This refers to the Jews who rejected the gospel message. They no longer had the right to call themselves "Jews" in the sense of being God's chosen people. They were Jews outwardly but not inwardly; physically but not spiritually (Galatians 3:26-29). **But do lie** is not included in the letter to Smyrna. It is added here for emphasis. The Jews' claim of spiritual superiority was a lie! **Worship before thy feet** is an expression that could be interpreted two ways: (1) Some of the Jews who now revile them would be converted to Christ. (2) When final judgment occurs the Jews will acknowledge Christ as Lord (Philippians 2:10-11) and the Christians will be vindicated. One thing is for sure — this does not mean the Jews would actually worship the Christians. God alone is to be worshipped (Matthew 4:10). **I have loved thee** indicates tender affection. Although Christ loves all people, he has a special relationship with the faithful because of their election.

The Lord's words in this verse "I will make them to come and worship before thy feet," are similar to the words of Isaiah (Isaiah 45:14; 49:23; 60:14), but with a twist. Isaiah depicted the Gentiles bowing before the Jews and acknowledging that God was with them. The Lord, however, states that the unbelieving Jews will bow before Christians and acknowledge that the Messiah loved them. Sweet vindication!

10) Because thou hast kept the word of my patience, I also will keep thee from the hour of temptation, which shall come upon all the world, to try them that dwell upon the earth.

Since the brethren have kept his word (v. 8), the Lord now promises to keep them from the hour of temptation. "Thou hast kept...I also will keep." Loyalty has its sure reward. **Patience** means endurance or perseverance. **Word of my patience** may refer to the teaching about the endurance that Christ requires or to the teaching about the endurance that Christ displayed. **Keep** comes from the Greek preposition *ek*, and can refer to either "immunity from" or "being brought safely through." The latter seems to fit the context of Revelation best. **Hour** indicates a full but limited period of testing. It is not to be taken literally. **Temptation** refers to a test or trial. The hour of temptation may refer to a period of increased persecution waged by Domitian or one of his successors.

The Lord promises that they will be brought safely through it. **Them that dwell upon the earth** is an expression found several times in the book of Revelation, and it always refers to unbelievers.

11) Behold, I come quickly: hold that fast which thou hast, that no man take thy crown.

I come quickly is probably not a reference to final judgment since it is not used that way in any of the other letters. It may refer to the Lord's coming in judgment against the unbelieving Jews in the city. **Hold fast** means to "keep hold of firmly." **Crown** comes from the Greek word *stephanos*, and refers to a victor's crown. It was the crown (or wreath) given to champions. This crown is also mentioned in the letter to Smyrna (2:10). There is a different Greek word for the crown of royalty *(diadema)*. **Take thy crown** is a metaphor for being disqualified in a contest. The idea is that of losing their salvation. The thought does not concern itself with gain to the taker but with loss to the loser.

The Lord exhorted the Philadelphians to "hold fast" lest their crown be taken away. Does that not imply that their crown could be taken away if they did not hold fast? Surely it does! This denies the once saved — always saved doctrine.

> **No one can ever take our crown from us, but by our own weakness or our own infidelity we ourselves can lose it (Barclay, p. 76)**

The two most persecuted churches, Smyrna and Philadelphia, were the most faithful, while the two least persecuted churches, Sardis and Laodicea, were the least faithful. This should serve as a warning to all churches of Christ that enjoy peace.

12) Him that overcometh will I make a pillar in the temple of my God, and he shall go no more out: and I will write upon him the name of my God, and the name of the city of my God, which is new Jerusalem, which cometh down out of heaven from my God: and I will write upon him my new name.

Pillar indicates permanence or stability. **He shall go no more out** would remind the brethren of their current living conditions. Philadelphia was a place of instability due to frequent earthquakes and tremors, which forced the people to evacuate the city. The Lord promises those who overcome that in their new city, the new Jerusalem, there will be no evacuations. *They will be given permanent residence!* **Temple** refers to heaven. **My God** appears four times in this verse, and demonstrates the close relationship that exists between the Father and Son (also see 3:2). Three precious inscriptions will be written upon the conqueror: (1) The name of God. (2) The name of the city of God. (3) The new name of Christ. **Name of my God** indicates possession or ownership. **Name of the city of my God** indicates citizenship or residence. The new Jerusalem is described at length in chapter 21. **My new name** indicates close association or fellowship with Christ. The idea of a new name would probably remind the brethren of the city, which had undergone several name changes (See introductory notes on Philadelphia).

13) He that hath an ear, let him hear what the Spirit saith unto the churches.

The Lord calls on each member to heed what the Spirit has said and promises them eternal life if they will do so. To hear is to obey.

LAODICEA

REVELATION 3:14-22

L aodicea was located about 45 miles southeast of Philadelphia in the Lycus River valley. It was about 6 miles from Hierapolis, 11 miles from Colossae, and 100 miles from Ephesus.

Laodicea was founded by Antiochus II and named after his wife, Laodice, whom he later divorced. After coming under Roman rule, Laodicea enjoyed the privilege of being a free city, meaning it was self-governed and not occupied by Roman troops.

Laodicea was an extremely prosperous city. It was situated at the junction of two important roads, which made it a powerful trading and commercial center. The city was notorious for its banking industry, black wool industry, and eye salve solution (called Phrygian powder), which was produced at a nearby medical school. Laodicea was also home to many wealthy retirees.

Laodicea was so prosperous that when an earthquake devastated the city during the reign of Emperor Nero (A. D. 60), the Laodiceans refused financial aid from Rome. Tacitus wrote, "Laodicea arose from the ruins by the strength of her own resources, and with no help from us."

Although Laodicea had many positives, it also had one big negative — lukewarm drinking water. It had to pipe in its water from several miles away through aqueducts. By the time the water reached the city, it was tepid. The water was not cold enough to be refreshing, like the stream water at Colossae, or hot enough to be relaxing, like the hot springs at Hierapolis. It was lukewarm, which made it good for nothing!

A significant Jewish population lived in Laodicea, but there is no mention of any persecution from them in the letter. In fact, there is no mention of any outside persecution in the letter.

Whereas Smyrna and Philadelphia received no condemnation in their letters, Laodicea received no commendation in its letter. There are no words of praise.

Nothing is known about the establishment of the church at Laodicea. We know that Paul was not the founder because he had never met them when he wrote to the Colossians (2:1), although he did write them a letter (4:16). Epaphras was probably the founder of the Laodicean church since he labored in the area (4:12-13).

3:14) And unto the angel of the church of the Laodiceans write; These things saith the Amen, the faithful and true witness, the beginning of the creation of God.

The Lord begins with another self-description. In this letter he describes himself as the Amen, the faithful and true witness, the beginning of the creation of God. **Amen** indicates truth. The idea is that of absolute truth; something firmly established. He is totally trustworthy. This is the only time that "Amen" appears in the Bible as a title, and may be an allusion to Isaiah 65:16, where God is twice called the "God of truth" (*amen* in Hebrew). Jesus is called "the faithful witness" in 1:5, meaning everything he speaks is undoubtedly true. **The beginning of the creation of God** refers to the fact that he was the origin or source of creation, the beginner (John 1:1-3; Colossians 1:16-18; Hebrews 1:1-2). This does not mean that he was the first created. The well-to-do brethren in Laodicea needed to know that Jesus was the source of all material things.

15) I know thy works, that thou art neither cold nor hot: I would thou wert cold or hot.

I know thy works indicates detailed knowledge of their actions. Nothing escapes his awareness. **Cold** comes from the Greek word *psuchros*, meaning freezing cold. **Hot** comes from the Greek word *zestos*, meaning boiling hot. Spiritually speaking, the Laodiceans were neither freezing cold nor boiling hot. They were somewhere in the middle. **I would thou wert cold** does not mean the Lord wanted them to be lost. He is simply saying that at least a cold person knows his condition, while a lukewarm person does not.

There are three spiritual temperatures — cold, hot, and lukewarm. Although human reasoning may think that it is better to be lukewarm than cold, the Lord says otherwise. He would rather someone be freezing cold and know he is lost than be lukewarm and not know he is lost.

16) So then because thou art lukewarm, and neither cold nor hot, I will spew thee out of my mouth.

Lukewarm would be all too familiar to those living in Laodicea. The city was notorious for its lukewarm drinking water. It was tepid and unbearable to drink. The Lord likened these brethren to their lukewarm water. **Spew thee out of my mouth** indicates repudiation or rejection. The idea is that of rejecting with extreme disgust. *Their spiritual condition made him sick!*

17) Because thou sayest, I am rich, and increased with goods, and have need of nothing; and knowest not that thou art wretched, and miserable, and poor, and blind, and naked.

The Laodiceans assessment of their condition was inaccurate. Things were not as they seemed. **I am rich** could refer to either their physical or spiritual condition, or both. Spiritually speaking, they were professors but not possessors. **Knowest not** indicates ignorance. Perhaps the worst thing about their condition was their ignorance of it. One is not inclined to fix a problem he does not know he has. **Poor** denotes complete destitution.

The first beatitude says, "Blessed are the poor in spirit, for theirs is the kingdom of heaven" (Matthew 5:3). The poor in spirit are those who are acutely aware of their spiritual poverty and their total dependence on God. There was none of this among the Laodiceans (Humble, pp. 97-98).

From a physical standpoint Smyrna was poor and Laodicea was rich. Yet the Lord pronounced Smyrna as rich and Laodicea as poor. This should serve as a warning to all churches of Christ that enjoy physical prosperity.

18) I counsel thee to buy of me gold tried in the fire, that thou mayest be rich; and white raiment, that thou mayest be clothed, and that the shame of thy nakedness do not appear; and anoint thine eyes with eyesalve, that thou mayest see.

Having diagnosed their true condition, the Great Physician now prescribes the remedy. **Buy of me** identifies the Lord as the source of true goods. He has what they need. *Those who needed nothing needed to buy something!* **Gold,** not the kind found in the banks in Laodicea, but the kind found in Christ. **Raiment,** not the kind made from the black wool of sheep in the fields, but the kind found in Christ. These robes are made white by "the blood of the Lamb" (7:14). **Eyesalve,** not the kind developed in the medical schools, but the kind found in Christ.

The connection between the Lord's counsel and the city itself is undeniable. The things he mentions are the very things Laodicea was most famous for — banking, black wool, and eye salve solution. Throughout the seven letters we have noted such connections.

19) As many as I love, I rebuke and chasten: be zealous therefore, and repent.

This verse is reminiscent of Proverbs 3:12 and Hebrews 12:6, although a different Greek word is used in the Hebrews text. The Lord's rebuke of the church was motivated by love. **Chasten** means discipline. **Zealous** means hot. The idea is that of boiling hot. To avoid being spewed out of the Lord's mouth, they needed to change their spiritual temperature from lukewarm to boiling hot.

The Laodiceans were told to repent of their lukewarm condition or the Lord would spew them out of his mouth. What if they did not repent? What if they were spewed out of his mouth? Would they still be saved? Surely not! This denies the once saved — always saved doctrine.

20) Behold, I stand at the door, and knock: if any man hear my voice, and open the door, I will come in to him, and will sup with him, and he with me.

I stand at the door and knock indicates exclusion. He was on the outside! He wants to come in and fellowship with them, but he must be let in first. **If any man hear my voice, and open the door** indicates individual responsibility. Each member is called upon to open the door. **Sup with him, and he with me** indicates individual association or fellowship (1 Corinthians 5:11; Galatians 2:12). The idea is that of dining in spiritual communion.

Some commentators see a link between the Lord being shut out and the city itself. A fortified gate had been built around the city which enabled the citizens to shut out unwelcome guests. Perhaps the Lord pictures himself as standing outside the gate of the church.

21) To him that overcometh will I grant to sit with me in my throne, even as I also overcame, and am set down with my Father in his throne.

Those who overcome can come over! They will be granted the privilege of sitting with Christ on his throne. Reigning with Christ is also promised to the conquerors in Thyatira (2:26-28). "To him that overcometh...even as I also overcame." The Lord has never asked us to do anything that he was not willing to do himself.

In each of the seven letters the Lord promises eternal life to those who overcome, though the figures differ. Ephesus was promised the tree of life in the paradise of God (2:7); Smyrna was promised escape from the second death (2:11); Pergamos was promised the hidden manna and a white stone with a secret name (2:17); Thyatira was promised authority over the nations and the morning star (2:26-27); Sardis was promised a white garment, their names in the book of life, and profession before the Father and angels (3:5); Philadelphia was promised to be made pillars in the temple of God, to be inscribed with the name of God, the name of the city of God, and the new name of Christ (3:12-13); and Laodicea was promised enthronement with Christ (3:21). These promises are still available to Christians today if they will overcome, but can only be achieved through perseverance.

22) He that hath an ear, let him hear what the Spirit saith unto the churches.

The Lord calls on each member to heed what the Spirit has said and promises them eternal life if they will do so. To hear is to obey.

CLOSING THOUGHTS

Although the letters to the seven churches of Asia were written centuries ago to people who lived on the other side of the globe, they are still applicable to us today. There are many valuable lessons to learn. Below are just a few closing thoughts to consider. They are in no particular order.

(1) Many churches pride themselves in being tolerant. They preach against all forms of judging and promise to accept anyone who will come their way — no questions asked. While tolerance is good in certain situations, it is by no means good in all situations. The Ephesians were commended because of their intolerance! They would not tolerate evil workers, false apostles, or the deeds of the Nicolaitans (2:2, 6), while those at Pergamos and Thyatira were criticized for tolerating those in error. Intolerance can be a good thing!

(2) Christians living in the province of Asia were social outcasts because they refused to worship the emperor or to participate in pagan festivals. The ostracism and rejection must have been difficult to bear at times. Yet they remained loyal to Christ. They did not buckle to peer pressure. Follow God, not men!

(3) Each church received its own letter from the Lord. He did not just send one letter to a "board" or "committee" that was responsible for overseeing the churches of that particular region. Each congregation acted as an autonomous and self-governing unit.

(4) Many churches today measure themselves by outward appearance. They think that beautiful buildings and large contributions equal spirituality. Not true! From Sardis we learn that it is certainly possible to be one thing externally and something altogether different internally. The same lesson can be learned from the other churches as well. True strength is not determined by outward appearance! A congregation's true strength is measured by how rich it is in faith.

(5) The two most persecuted churches, Smyrna and Philadelphia, were the most faithful, while the two least persecuted churches, Sardis and Laodicea, were the least faithful. This proves that adversity can be a good thing. As James wrote, "the trying of your faith worketh patience!"

(6) The seven letters remind us that it does matter what members of the church believe and practice. Those who held to the false doctrines of the Nicolatians, Balaam, and Jezebel were condemned even though they had obeyed the gospel. Doctrine matters!

(7) Many churches refuse to practice discipline. They turn a blind eye and deaf ear to sin. This approach may not "rock the boat" but it will "sink the ship!" Those at Pergamos and Thyatira were criticized by the Lord for not taking

disciplinary action against those who were espousing error in their midst. The Lord will not tolerate the spirit of compromise. Such people must be expelled in order to keep the church pure (Romans 16:17; 1 Corinthians 5:9-11; 2 Thessalonians 3:6, 14-15; Titus 3:10). Discipline is a good thing!

(8) The devil is real! He will use whatever resources he can to attack Christians, including civil government (like Rome), other religions (like Judaism and paganism), and even erring members of the church (like the Nicolaitans, Balaamites, and Jezebel). Know your enemy!

(9) We hear a lot of denominational preachers lifting up the nation of Israel as if the Jews are still God's chosen people, even though they have rejected his Son. How can that be considering the fact that the unbelieving Jews were twice called "a synagogue of Satan" in the seven letters? The Lord said their claim of spiritual superiority was a "lie" (3:9). True Israel is spiritual, not physical!

(10) It is interesting to note how much of the letters addressed issues — problems in the church, dangers facing the church, etc. The same can be said about most of the epistles in the New Testament. For instance, Paul's first epistle to the Corinthians addressed division, immorality, marriage and divorce, liberty, the roles of men and women, the Lord's Supper, spiritual gifts, the resurrection, and stewardship. He addressed one issue after another. Preachers should not shy away from dealing with issues!

(11) Although a Christian can have confidence that he is saved, it is possible to cast away that confidence (Hebrews 10:35). It is possible for those who have "escaped the pollutions of the world through the knowledge of the Lord and Savior Jesus Christ" to "turn from the holy commandment delivered unto them" (2 Peter 2:20-21).

(12) There is no attempt in the seven letters to explain away the reality of evil or the afflictions it causes Christians. Nor are there any promises to remove the difficulties. Unlike the "prosperity preachers" of today, the Lord does not blame their problems on a "lack of faith" or promise smooth sailing if they will only contribute more money when the plate is passed. Christians are not exempt from suffering!

(13) The members at Laodicea were apparently prosperous and self-dependent. They were also spiritually indifferent. They had shut the Lord out of their assembly without even knowing it. Sound familiar? That sounds just like many churches in America. Take heed, brethren!

(14) The Lord called on the brethren at Smyrna to be faithful even if it meant death (2:10). This was no more than what he had been willing to do. Jesus has never asked us to do anything that he was not willing to do himself (3:21)!

(15) The Lord ended each letter with a call for the members to "hear" what the Spirit said. As noted, to hear is to obey. Only those who are obedient to the will of God have the hope of heaven (22:14).

(16) The Lord's longsuffering and mercy is evident throughout the seven letters. Even when dealing with Jezebel, the Lord said, "I gave her space to repent" (2:21) and then pleaded with her one last time to do so.

(17) The deity of Christ is affirmed over and over again in the seven letters. He is described as eternal, ominscient, omnipotent, and omnipresent.

(18) Christ expects total commitment. It is clearly evident that status-quo is not acceptable to the Lord. It is not enough to sit in the pew and just go through the motions. He wants whole-hearted followers who are willing to sweat!

(19) The Lord wasted no time getting to the point in each of the seven letters. Too many preachers today "beat around the bush" in their sermons rather than just saying what needs to be said. Get to the point!

(20) Each of the seven letters emphasize the importance of perseverance. Only those who finish their course victoriously will be rewarded. The race must be won!

(21) No lesson is more obvious in the seven letters than this one: THE LORD IS WATCHING! He is still walking among the churches inspecting them with a close eye. *He knows our works!*

www.ingramcontent.com/pod-product-compliance
Lightning Source LLC
Chambersburg PA
CBHW071906020426
42331CB00010B/2700